YOUR KNOWLEDGE HAS VALUE

- We will publish your bachelor's and
  master's thesis, essays and papers

- Your own eBook and book -
  sold worldwide in all relevant shops

- Earn money with each sale

Upload your text at www.GRIN.com
and publish for free

Amos Kamau

Leading change at Corus

GRIN Verlag

Bibliografische Information der Deutschen Nationalbibliothek:

Die Deutsche Bibliothek verzeichnet diese Publikation in der Deutschen National-
bibliografie; detaillierte bibliografische Daten sind im Internet über http://dnb.d-
nb.de/ abrufbar.

Imprint:

Copyright © 2012 GRIN Verlag GmbH
Druck und Bindung: Books on Demand GmbH, Norderstedt Germany
ISBN: 978-3-656-55483-7

This book at GRIN:

http://www.grin.com/en/e-book/265518/leading-change-at-corus

GRIN - Your knowledge has value

Der GRIN Verlag publiziert seit 1998 wissenschaftliche Arbeiten von Studenten, Hochschullehrern und anderen Akademikern als eBook und gedrucktes Buch. Die Verlagswebsite www.grin.com ist die ideale Plattform zur Veröffentlichung von Hausarbeiten, Abschlussarbeiten, wissenschaftlichen Aufsätzen, Dissertationen und Fachbüchern.

Visit us on the internet:

http://www.grin.com/

http://www.facebook.com/grincom

http://www.twitter.com/grin_com

Introduction

The business environment has become very dynamic making change in organizations inevitable and tremendous in past few decades. Leadership through change has thus become a great concern in today's business management (Axelrod 2000, p. 43). Managing change effectively is important in keeping change efforts in track and overcoming business challenges. In addition, modern organizations are highly complex and cannot be transformed by one management guru. Leadership effort must therefore support and build organization members particularly employees to understand leadership agenda in managing change and play their role within the sphere of their activities (Black & Hal 2002, p. 91). Implementing change sometimes require sense of urgency. Of great importance is to understand change, drivers and barriers of change and identify strategies and initiatives geared towards leading change effectively. This study explores and examines changes that have occurred at Corus, how the company has managed them, barriers that have been faced concerning change and reasons for the changes.

Corus

Tata Steel Group is world's sixth largest producer of steel. Corus forms part of the group in Europe being the second largest producer of steel in Europe with approximately £12 billion annual revenue. Corus produces over 20 million tons annually in U.K. and in Netherlands. The company has global network of service centres and sales offices employing about 42,000 staff across globe (Corus, 2010). Corus has been a leader in supplying steel to various markets across the globe. Long Products Business is Corus' business unit that manufactures steel in France, Scotland and England. The three units produce various steel products that range from wire rod to steel plate to steel rail. Key markets for the Long Products Business include engineering, construction, mining, machinery, earthmoving equipments, fastening, rail and ship building. Continuous improvement gives business a competitive advantage enabling it to stick ahead of its competitors and also increase market share. Good use of experience and skills enables organizations to enhance better products and processes. In the context of Corus, the company uses continuous improvement to drive new and innovative products development and meet customers' needs (Corus, 2010). Continuous improvement practices have enabled Corus to solve problems that face its steel works and win great contracts. Continuous improvement practices coupled with the dynamic market environment gives forth to new products development and changes in the business process across the company's divisions and department. Corus is thus challenge to come up with a way of managing the inevitable change.

External environment operated in keeps on changing and businesses are challenged to respond on time and appropriately to the changes faced in order to secure their competitiveness. Change management requires support from various business stakeholders including management, employees, shareholders and suppliers among others. Such cooperation ensures that the changes made remain embedded to the shaping of the firm. In the context of Corus, the company launched a culture plan through the Corus Strip Products or the CSP team in UK (Corus, 2010). This plan focused on change management and was dubbed 'The Journey'. The aims of the company were to address wide business challenges and how people carried out work. The plan focused on beliefs and values of the organization members as well as suppliers and partners. The eight core values defined by the plan guides Corus and offer its members the guiding principles. CSP Journey outlined behaviours and values that Corus expected members to follow and encouraged them to remain accountable. Some of the issues the plan aimed at eliminating included tragic accidents occurring on site among other safety and health issues. CSP Journey underpins the company's culture and has given Corus U.K. a positive approach.

Reasons for change

Change in organizations involves four major components; these include drivers for change, barriers to change, creation and implementation of change and measuring effectiveness of change. Drivers of change are internal and external forces of change in an organization. At Corus, internal forces include safety and health issues while external forces include company's growing strength of the competitors (Kotter 1996, p. 43). To identify drivers for change, staff is made to understand what is happening in every aspect of the business and identify any existing flaws. To identify barriers, staff attitudes are critically important and must often be evaluated. Creating and implementing change plan focuses on winning staff commitment, identifying possible solutions to problem areas and identifying ways of measuring the improvements made. To measure effectiveness of measure is critical, CSP uses this component to ensure that further changes are made based on outcomes of previous actions.

Drivers of change at Corus

Internal drivers

Internal drivers include inefficiencies occurring within the business (Dyer 1984, p. 63). Some of the internal inefficiencies identified by CSP at Corus included poor delivery where Corus incurred delays in delivering steel to the customers, which led to losses in business. Competitiveness was also a key issue, Corus steel produced in U.K. proved more expensive that that produced from other countries. There was also high wastage particularly arising from failure to make required quality, which required reworking on the products or scraping them. Another key internal problem faced by Corus was low staff morale whereby employees were committed but they lacked motivation in the workplace.

External drivers of change

These are pressure that organizations face demanding change, which arise from factors outside the organization (Conner 1998, p. 82). In the case of Corus, some of the external pressures for change included new competitors; these are low cost producers that minimized demand for high-cost producers like Corus. Changing customer requirements including reduced demand for steel used in automotive industry implied that the company required building other customer segments and other products. New technology used in production also played a key role in changing demand as customers expected high specifications. In addition market perception of steel industry was slowly becoming negative. For instance, steel industry was deemed poor in environmental concerns.

Management of change

Various approaches to change management can be adapted including power-coercive, environmental adaptive, normative reductive and empirical rational. Environmental adaptive assumes that people oppose disruptions and loss but they adapt to new circumstances readily. With that assumption change is enhanced by gradually transferring members from old ways to the new ways of doing things (Nickols, 2010). The approach is best suited where transformative and radical change is required, where gradual change is necessary, this strategy is not suitable (Conner 1992, p. 56). Power-coercive strategy assumes that people will be compliant and authority is vital in enhancing change through imposition of sanctions. Where there is eminent threat that requires drastic change, this strategy proves suitable. Normative-reductive strategy assumes that people are social and thus adhere to cultural values and norms and that successful change can thus be attained through redefining existing values and norms and exercising commitment. This strategy focuses on culture. Empirical-rational strategy of change assumes that people are rational and thus follow self-interest (Kirkpatrick 1985, p. 102). The strategy view is that change is successfully attained through communication of information as well as through incentives perceived. This change strategy focuses on balancing incentives and the risk management. In selecting the best change management strategy, consideration is given to various factors including degree of resistance, degree of change, the members involved and the stakes.

Managing change at Corus

Total quality management

Change management at Corus takes environment-adaptive change strategy where members are assumed to adapt to new ways readily. Corus Strip Products or the CSP has implemented Total Quality Management or the TQM initiatives that focused improving productivity and competitiveness. Corus has initially reduced workforce but being a company with deeply committed workforce and low staff turnover, the company realized that it made more sense enabling workforce to be more efficient rather than reducing the number of staff. TQM provides fundamental structure for quality focused and customer-oriented continuous improvements at Corus. Key elements of TQM as practiced at Corus include policy management, daily management and tasking achieving through problem solving. Policy management at Corus is a structured strategy that focuses on development and deployment processes. Daily management is a structure methodology that is used to conduct activities on regular basis ensuring that job efficiency is attained among the operating employees. Task achieving through problem solving is a structure methodology that is used to identify root causes of problems and ways of solving them in order to accomplish major tasks. Corus uses TQM to enhance continuous performance improvements. The company conducts audits using both internal and external auditors, which helps in identifying areas of improvement. This has enabled Corus to achieve considerable improvements in various areas.

Continuous improvements

Continuous improvement involves making small continuous improvements in business functions, processes and systems. Continuous improvements also involve empowering people to make effective decisions to enhance internal capabilities and improve quality and that way meet customers' needs. These continuous improvement practices identify areas where there is waste through support of lean production, such improvements help reduce costs related to wastes at Corus. Lean production is done where waste is minimized, work flow is smooth and there is focus on customers' needs. Lean production makes use of few resources and applies them efficiently to improve productivity and profitability. At Corus, continuous improvements help in eliminating waste in seven most important areas including transport, inventory, motion, defects, waiting times, over production and over processing. In transport, improvement has involved reducing size and weight of pieces of materials to ease handling. Inventory management improvement has involved ensuring that relevant customer outlets are made available to avoid building up of stocks. Effective project planning has been important in ensuring efficient performance thus avoiding unnecessary movement of people and goods. Timescales and equipments are planned ahead to reduce waiting times. Unnecessary steps in processing are also eliminated to avoid over processing while computer modelling is applied to reduce number of required trails when seeking to obtain suitable results and this eliminates over production. Computer modelling also helps in minimizing trial failures and this reduces defects. Corus makes use of Just In Time (JIT) in inventory management, which allows the company to hold just-enough finished goods to meet the current demand and the least amount of stock of raw materials.

Continuous improvement as part of total quality management strategy at Corus has influenced the whole business to become effective. All employees must however be encouraged to own the principles of continuous improvement and adopt them starting with the senior management to the junior staff for continuous improvement to be attained throughout the organization. Strong communication is vital and it plays an important role in enhancing commitment (Galpin 1996, p. 32). Regular presentations of CI have been vital in communicating the practices to the staff. The company's management has also made use of newsletters and team briefings as a way of ensuring that the practices to staff. Employees are encouraged to contribute ideas that can improve work practices and the company's competitiveness in the steel industry. Continuous improvement makes Corus not only more efficient but also offers benefits to stakeholders including governments, Royal Navy, customers and Lloyds Shipping Register who get high quality products and materials of high specification.

Product development

Corus explore new product developments through contracts. For instance, new aircraft carriers, which need high specification has challenged Corus to explore an opportunity for new product development. Ideas for product development rise from competitors, innovations, changes in technologies and employees. New products development is one of way of managing change at Corus. Competition challenges the company to develop new products in response to the competitors. Technologies change and its effects challenges companies like Corus to invest in research and development in order to identify new applications in production and business processes (Heller 1998, p. 121). Innovations play a critically important role at Corus in enabling the company get new ideas that guide them in making new products. Continuous improvements have been effective in enabling Corus address the various external and internal sources of pressure including competition, changing customer needs and wastes. The strategy has enabled Corus develop new steel products at competitive price since there is cost efficiency. The strategy has also minimized cost of manufacturing and enabled Corus to meet customers' demand and adhere to their deadlines. Continuous improvements have also enabled Corus to adopt best practices in the steel industry, which has facilitated overall improvement of performance.

Barriers to change

When change occurs in organization, people's abilities, customs, practices and experiences are challenged. It may therefore be deemed as threat to the existing order and thus be received with resistance particularly where job roles are changed, jobs are cut and descriptions altered (Scott & Dennis 1995, p. 96). Change can therefore lead to low work morale among staff and thus lead to poor performance and poor productivity (Kanter et al 1992, p. 106). In the context of Corus, although CSP had managed to deliver change and bring about innovation, not all the programmes involved produced the desired results. As a company in a traditional industry, Corus had its own patterns of carrying out business and the culture engraved made it difficult to alter the way the employees were used to doing things. Some employees deemed the new business initiatives as threats to their teams and also to their positions. Job reduction in the steel industry was not a new theme since 1970s and also within Corus in its previous change initiatives that had led to reduction of workforce. This gave employees the fear of losing their jobs.

Other members of the workforce saw no threat of the change since they were used to Corus overcoming difficult times in the past. Such complacency however made change management difficult at Corus (Kotter & Dan 2002, p. 74). The other critical issue was the company's ageing workforce who had high technical skills that were not easily transferable. This made the industry less attractive to young people due to reduced apprenticeship schemes and reduced job opportunities. The other barrier to the change desired at Corus was the long history of the company in rewarding long service as opposed to distinguished service. The company felt that this areas required change and was ready to start rewarding staff with higher output.

Overcoming barriers

Corus realized that it could not overcome the challenges faced by reducing workforce or by increasing investment. The only way out was changing how they carried out business. One way of overcoming staff resistance to the change was by working closely with staff and involving them in the continuous improvement programme. Corus shared with the workforce on the effects of not changing the way they carried out business and encouraged staff to won the change and the new values by signing up to the change programme. This saw employees adapt the change and participate in decision making. Their experience and contributions were recognized (Black & Hal 2002, p. 64). Effective communication was also recognized as critical and Corus communicated on weekly basis to the staff through workshops, and weekly newsletters. Such communication was essential in ensuring that employees' behaviours are aligned with the communicated values including professionalism, excellence, improvement, respect, honesty, integrity, fairness and transparency. These values were focused on helping employees who were willing to improve performance if given assistance.

Measuring change outcomes

To evaluate change and its effects, it is important to identify key performance indicators that will be used to measure outcomes (Skarke et al 1995, p. 87).The change implemented at Corus has contributed to sustainability of business through facing up the internal weaknesses. Corus has improved output production, efficiency, cost reduction and waste reduction in the increasingly competitive market. The change has not only led to survival but also growth. Corus worked to established standards and targets as well as milestones for everyone, which made it easier for the company to review progress and measure outcomes. Key performance indicators included increasing production capacity to five million tons and achieving 20% cost reduction in steel production. Other KPIs included reduction of absenteeism improved customer service quality, tighter safety and health targets and reduced carbon monoxide emissions. The company's teams, departments and individuals have supported improvement culture. The staff are more committed in achieving the company targets and values.

Conclusion

Change is necessary for organizations to remain competitive and continually achieve their objectives and goals. Failure to change and effectively manage change makes companies to be left in competition (Bridges 1991, p. 72). From a consultant view, Corus has been successful in pointing out the issues that need change and confronting change barriers. This has been critical in enabling the company to win commitment and support of staff, and also in delivering effective change. Various initiatives employed by Corus including total quality management and continuous improvement practices have been vital in creating the desired change and allowing for continued improvement. Performance improvement has also earned the company more government grants in support to the steel production in U.K. as one of the important economic sectors.

9

References

Axelrod, R (2000), *Terms of Engagement: Changing The Way We Change Organizations,* San Francisco, California, Berrett-Koehler Publishers, Inc.

Black, J & Hal, B (2002), *Leading Strategic Change,* Upper Saddle River, New Jersey, Financial Times Prentice Hall.

Bridges, W (1991), *Managing Transitions: Making The Most Of Change,* Reading, Massachusetts, Perseus Books.

Conner, D (1998), *Leading At The Edge Of Chaos: How To Create The Nimble Organization,* New Jersey, John Wiley & Sons, Inc.

Conner, D (1992), *Managing At The Speed Of Change.* New York, Villard Books.

Corus (2010), *Overcoming barriers to change.* Retrieved from: http://www.google.co.ke/url?sa=t&rct=j&q=&esrc=s&source=web&cd=1&ved=0CC IQFjAA&url=http%3A%2F%2Fbusinesscasestudies.co.uk%2Fcorus%2Fovercoming-barriers-to-change%2Fconclusion.html&ei=6MlxT5btD6PM0QXHhMAH&usg=AFQjCNFLrfsq tJ2hw1-JzjmpEp93bZrTZQ.

Dyer, W (1984), *Strategies For Managing Change,* Reading, Massachusetts, Addison-Wesley Publishing Company, Inc.

Galpin, T (1996), *The Human Side of Change,* San Francisco, California, Jossey-Bass Inc., Publishers.

Heller, R (1998), *Managing Change,* New York, DK Publishing, Inc.

ILM (2005) *Management Extra:* Change Management, New York, Elsevier

Kanter, R, Barry, A & Todd, D (1992), *The Challenge Of Organizational Change,* New York, The Free Press.

Kirkpatrick, D (1985), *How To Manage Change Effectively,* San Francisco, California, Jossey-Bass Inc., Publishers.

Kotter, J & Dan, S (2002), *The Heart of Change,* Boston, Massachusetts, Harvard Business School Press.

Kotter, J (1996), *Leading Change,* Boston, Massachusetts, Harvard Business School Press.

Nickols, F (2010), *Four change management strategies.* Retrieved from: http://www.google.co.ke/url?sa=t&rct=j&q=&esrc=s&source=web&cd=1&ved=0CC

10

IQFjAA&url=http%3A%2F%2Fwww.nickols.us%2Ffour_strategies.pdf&ei=z39xT9
v-MtSA8gPKgqVK&usg=AFQjCNEtZwmOKH3UIuGEvYVPS3vrrbvaTw

Scott, C & Dennis, T (1995), *Managing Change At Work: Leading People Through Organizational Transitions,* Menlo Park, California, Crisp Publications, Inc.

Skarke, G, Butch, H, Bill, R & Diane, L (1995), *The Change Management Toolkit: A Step-By-Step Methodology For Successfully Implementing Dramatic Organizational Change,* Second Edition. Houston, Texas, WinHope Press.